Angels & Waterfalls

The MYSTERY of MIRACLES
THROUGH THE REVELATION OF HIS VOICE

DARCEL STEWART

ACKNOWLEDGEMENTS

Charles, my husband you were the first to tell me to write about the miracles that have transpired in my life because you witnessed a lot of them yourself. Thank you for inspiring me.

To my children Raquel (Jason), Charles (Mira), Sidney (Celeste) and Lia (Allen) you are my pride and joy. I love you so very much. Savanna, Jason Jr. Sophia, Josiah, Judah and Eden, yet in the womb, my grandchildren you bless my soul.

To my mother, you are my best friend forever. Dad I miss you. I thank God for you all and your role in blessing my life.

CONTENTS

1

Purpose

Who follows the path of a waterfall? We enjoy the majestic sight before us, allowing ourselves to question if at all, only momentarily, the origin or the destination of each crystal. The sweet slippery sound of water satiating a welcoming hillside, twirling and twisting through the early morning dawn and the spicy evening dusk is soothing to the soul. I liken it to the voice of God.

Imagine that every drop of the fall has a contemplated end, and that every drop, through the journey has an identified purpose. Tumultuous turns through raggedy rocks, to the naked eye makes the Fall that much more imposing. We are forced to inhale the regal oxygen dancing around the Fall and then exhale "aw" as we stand still and yet step as close to the beckoning water as it will allows us to do so.

Angels & Waterfalls is a narrative non-fiction spiritually charged journey through the miracles that have taken place in my life as a result of my being able to discern the voice of God. I am not claiming to be any more than I am, just a willing vessel and a living testimony that the Lord speaks to us. The events depicted in this memoir are just trinkets of a life that is in conversation with the Lord on a moment to moment basis.

Angels are as mysterious to mankind as waterfalls are beautiful to him. We can't figure them out, we just know that they exist. They represent the nature of God and His presence in our lives. He is the great mystery who allows us to take the path set before us as the water that falls down the welcoming slope does.

Angels & Waterfalls takes the everyday challenges that we all face and shows us how our dependence on God and the guidance and protection from His precious Angels can keep us from making a catastrophic detour to a spiritual or physical death. A life without twists and turns is not promised to any of us. As a matter of fact, our final destination is upon us, with its uncertainty in every breath that we take. Angels & Waterfalls demonstrates that the Lord knows our voice. How much more purposeful our lives would be if only we could recognize His.

The Purpose Driven Life by Rick Warren catapulted my belief that every given moment in my life has a purpose. Doorways to Deception by Mac Hammond showed me how subtle and foreboding pride can be as it enters and prances on our being, taking over our lives in crevices that we barely knew existed. The Bait of Satan by John Bevere assisted me in dismantling the spirit of revenge that was festering in my spirit as I was being bullied on my job by a supervisor. Tuesdays with Morrie by Mitch Albom represents the personalities that foster our plan and our purpose to be that which God intended no matter how insignificant. Fate of the

Seed by Sidney Stewart places the burden on that which we plant to ultimately grow and replicate that which is worthy of respect. Angels & Waterfalls will quench the thirst of the person who is trying to make sense out of a life that does not make sense to the modern world.

I have taught high school literature for almost thirty years. I have also mentored hundreds of young ladies through a program that I sponsor at my church as well as my school. As a servant of the Lord and a Pastor's wife, I have mentored countless women and have served on various auxiliaries. I have often been told that I have a pipeline to heaven and that I must write my experiences down. I have attempted to start the conversation with a few of them in Angels & Waterfalls.

2

Evidence

People who are aware of their spiritual gifts, walk in the purpose that God has destined, for them. Those who do not, wander in the wilderness without a purpose or clear direction. We edify God best when we use our body as a living sacrifice, blessing others as we embrace the blessings that He has bestowed upon us.

My hope is that the evidence of God's voice be revealed in the hearts of man. God is constantly speaking to His children. Whether we know it or not, we are responding to His voice with either "yes" and "no," all the time. How much more fulfilling our lives would be if we recognized His voice, and walked according to His purpose? Having a true relationship with God means never having to ask Him why, because no matter what happens, you know that it is going to work together for *"the good of those who love Him, who have been called according to His purpose"* (*Romans 8:28*).

People would not dread going to work, married couples would not be living in an emotional hell, fathers would not abandon their children and children would respect their parents, if they understood that as mysterious as angels are to man and as whimsical as waterfalls are to nature such as that we all are in the scheme of God's plan. We exist for His joy, His pleasure and His purpose.

Our walk is only in vain if it lacks His guidance. Imagine if you can, the path of the countless numbers of water drops that comprise a waterfall. How difficult is it to look away from the rushing water? We are mesmerized by the beauty of the unmistaken journey that the water is taking. Yet, the water is doing nothing but taking the path set before her. As a Pastor's wife, mother of four, grandmother of six, mentor of hundreds of teenage girls over the years, high school teacher of thousands I have witnessed lives spiral out of control. Questions we often ask ourselves, "How did I get here, why is this happening to me, what did I do wrong, when will I get out of this, surface in the subtle corners of our thoughts when we realize that we should have followed our "first mind." Had I known all of this I would not have married her. If only I had turned at that other corner, we would be there by now. If I had called him last night this would not have happened! The regrets, the regrets, the regrets that swirl around in our heads, when we find ourselves trying to dig our way out of sinking sand.

Think about it. We gravitate towards energy that we want in our lives, whether it is people, movies, books or even restaurants. When and where we feel that we have choices we choose accordingly. What we let in, we often let out in some way, shape or form. If we only see bad eating habits, that is often what we mimic. If our parents and our neighbors or maybe even our friends or coworkers end their marriage, divorce becomes an option for us.

In order to get what God has for us, we must be able to recognize His voice. But in order to do that, we must flush out the filth that is naturally within us, keeping us in bondage, blinding us from His path, obstructing our view of His promises. If we are holding anger in our heart for someone, we will not be able to get a prayer through to the Lord to lead, to guide and to direct us. We must humble our heart and pray for forgiveness for harboring anger, jealousy, lust and pride. We are obligated to let the Lord know, that as difficult as it is to let go of this trash, we honestly want to do it. We want to be free of iniquity, so that we can hear from Him. We can refuse to be a victim of our circumstances and choose to be victorious over them!

[4] *For whatsoever is born of God overcometh the world: and this is the victory that overcometh the world, even our faith. 1 John 5:4*

3

EARLIEST RECOGNITION OF FAITH

[11]And I beheld, and I heard the voice of many angels round about the throne and the beasts and the elders: and the number of them was ten thousand times ten thousand, and thousands of thousands; [12]Saying with a loud voice, Worthy is the Lamb that was slain to receive power, and riches, and wisdom, and strength, and honour, and glory, and blessing. Revelation 5:11-12

Between the mystery of the wind, the stillness of the night and the brilliance of the moon I found unspeakable peace. Somewhere out there my God existed. I knew that wherever some-where was, that it was the most awesome place in the universe to be. The view of the stars from my bedroom window is the earliest connection to God that I can remember. The depth of a seemingly "no-where-ness" infatuated me so much to the point that I could not release my eyes from its inescapable glory. By the age of six, I had become accustomed to the "Now I lay me down to sleep, pray the Lord my soul to keep" request that my mother helped my sister and brothers and I make, but for some reason the words were more than just a sing-song nightly ritual to me.

I grew up in the red and brown brick Herman Garden Projects on Detroit city's west side in the early nineteen sixties until about the mid-nineteen seventies. My parents were high school sweethearts and they found themselves married as teenagers, having my brother and myself in the same year, just ten months apart. They would have my sister a year and a half later and my younger brother four years after that. Needless-to-say, they had their hands full at a very young age. One desire they had for us, their children, was that we were educated by the best means possible. So, they enrolled us in a parochial school outside of our inner-city project. My mother was raised Catholic and my father Baptist although I have never known my father to attend any church on a regular basis.

We were required to attend mass once a week during the school day with our classroom teacher. "Avayyy Avayyy Mareeeeaaaah" is the song that resonates in my mind as I see myself entering the maroon carpeted and marble floored sanctuary that hosted sandy brown stained pews with maroon kneelers and song books on either end of the bench. Picture perfect ponytails and burgundy and grey pleated uniforms sheathed starch white blouses and sleepy flamed lit candles, are speckled through my memory as the standard of that day.

Not long after the class was seated the mass would start. I can't say that I remember any message, or that one scripture stood out any more than another, but there was just something special about being in the presence of an awesome God. The air seemed lighter, even the sun's rays intruding the gold, red and blue stained church windows appeared purposeful. Everything was decent and in order and in the perfect-ness was the magnificence of the Almighty God. It was on those early Tuesday mornings, rain or shine, where other elementary school students were probably clapping their hands to a nursery rhyme or trying to decide which shoe to tie first or which crayon to put in the pencil box, that I was being exposed to the Father, the Son and the Holy Spirit.

My earliest encounter with an expectation of faith was sometime into my second or third grade year. My classmates and I had an opportunity to put our head down on the desk and rest for a few minutes. I really wanted a pumpkin seed so much to the point that I could almost taste the salt, and I really believed without the shadow of a doubt, that God could make it happen for me, in that moment. I kept praying for the pumpkin seed to appear in my hand, but it never did. God had decided that I did not need a pumpkin seed at that time and I eventually accepted His no response. But His saying no, not right now, did not lessen the faith that I had in His ability to do anything He wants to do, whenever He wants to do it. I thank my parents for introducing God to me through prayer.

[13] *People were bringing little children to Jesus for him to place his hands on them, but the disciples rebuked them.* [14] *When Jesus saw this, he was indignant. He said to them, "Let the little children come to me, and do not hinder them, for the kingdom of God belongs to* such as these. [15] *Truly, I tell you, anyone who will not receive the kingdom of God like a little child will never enter it." [16] And he took the children in his arms, placed his hands on them and blessed them. Mark 10:13-16*

Allow the Lord to speak into your life.
Make His way your way.
Pray blessings on the child in your womb.
Show your children that God is important to you all the time.

[6] *Train up a child in the way he should go: and when he is old, he will not depart from it. Proverbs 22:6*

4

Noisome Pestilence

He that dwelleth in the secret place of the most High shall abide under the shadow of the Almighty. I will say of the Lord, He is my refuge and my fortress: my God; in him will I trust. Surely he shall deliver thee from the snare of the fowler, and from the noisome pestilence...Psalm 91

I attended a high school thirty-five minutes from my home, in the downtown area of Detroit in the 1970's. Because of its superior academic standards, the school was known to house four thousand of the city's brightest and best students. Transportation was the responsibility of the parent or student, so I had to catch the city bus along with hundreds of my schoolmates.

Grand River was an extremely busy street on the west side at the time. There was a department store called Federals and another one across the street called Montgomery Wards. I remember waiting on the Grand River bus in front of my school one blistery cold December afternoon. I cannot recall why my two best friends were not at the bus stop that day, but my normal routine would slightly change because of their absence. I ended up taking the Fenkell bus, which ran east, west instead of the Grand River bus, because it arrived first. By the time my bus reached the point at which I was to transfer, the sidewalk had become somewhat slippery, which would not have been an issue had I not worn my diva suede three-inch heel boots to school that day. My maxi coat kept me warm, but my toes were starting to freeze because I had missed the connecting bus.

As cold as it was, I started to walk the half mile home heading north on Greenfield, a major street on the west side of Detroit. I happen to naturally glance from time to time at the cars whizzing by me this busy weekday afternoon. I caught the eyes of a man driving and looking at me while I was making my way up the street, which would not have been so odd in and of itself. because men look at women, that is normal, but it was a man of a different race who appeared to be middle aged. I continued to make my way, trying not to slip on a patch of ice or trip over unleveled pavement. Moments later, I saw the same guy, driving north this time. I tried to act as if I had not noticed him because there were hundreds of cars on the road. But my spirit at the young age of 15 would not let me rest. I made my way to the next main street which was Puritan. I could have taken that way to my street, should have taken that way to my street, but I did not follow my first mind…that still small voice.

I had not seen the guy for about ten minutes and my reasoning for not walking down Puritan was that it was so open that it would be easy for the guy to see where I lived, which I now realize made no sense at all. I walked up the block to the next side street hoping that I would not feel the negative spirit of that man again. I got to the middle of block, looking down at the wet pavement most of the time to stay clear of the ice patches. Low and behold, a blue four door vehicle pulled up to the corner which was about 30 feet away from me. The man who had been driving up and down Greenfield watching me was now leaning over the passenger seat to open the door. He beckoned me to get in his car. Realizing that I ignored the voice in me to go down Puritan a busy street to take an isolated street home was the worst thing that I could have done under the circumstances. I had those three-inch heels on, in the middle of the street at the foot of an alley, on a sidewalk riddled with ice. I looked behind me for any sign of life. I looked in front of me praying to see an approaching vehicle.

Nothing but the stillness of cold and the ill will of this man, was stirring on Florence Street. Beside me was a tall wooden fence, enclosing the yard that led to the house that I could have run to, banged on the door and gotten help from someone. I was about to be kidnapped by a middle-aged white man driving a blue four door vehicle in my black middle-class neighborhood, three blocks away from my home.

Had he run up to me and shoved me in his car I would have been a casualty, a missing teen, a victim of rape. There was no doubt in my mind that my frozen toes and those heels would not get my body back to the main road without my falling. I started screaming as if I saw someone coming. I screamed as loudly as I could, I waved my hands wildly and I prayed. There was no one, absolutely no one in sight, but he looked to his left and as if he had seen someone, he looked back at me closed the passenger door and drove down the street.

I made my way home, still shaken, lifeless toes, but safe at home. I described the man to my mother detailing the tumultuous experience. She called the police.

Decades later, I would hear about the teen murders that took place in Oakland County in the late 1970's. The first time I saw the unsolved cold case documentary, a feeling of uneasiness overcame me. I realized that the girls disappeared around the same time that I was being stalked by that man. It was as if I could feel that man's spirit again, see him motioning me to come closer, to get in his car. Whether or not it was the same man, they shared the same ominous spirit. That the young girls were abducted between 1976 and 1977 in the winter months was more than a coincidence. Had my eyes not connected to his soul, I could have walked right up to the car to cross the street right in front of him.

I have often told my daughters and the young ladies that I teach and, or mentor that someone is always watching you. I tell them that you cannot be so pre-occupied with your phones or your purses or even your friends, that you are not aware of your surroundings. But, recognizing the devil in a smiling face, takes spiritual aptitude. Spiritual aptitude is a gift rewarded to the believer who is in relationship with God.

Examine your heart.
Make positive intentions today.
Pray for your adversaries, one soul at a time.
Repent.

I applied for and secured a job at a restaurant called Arthur Treacher's Fish and Chips in the Rosedale Park subdivision. The area was a working-class neighborhood and considered safe and family friendly at the time. My peers were no more than sixteen to twenty-one years old so working was just fun for us and a means for buying All Star (gym shoes) and the cutest purses we could find to carry to school.

One evening, a male customer caught my attention. I could not tell you how he looked or what he was wearing. There was nothing distinguishing about him, but his spirit spoke volumes. He had ordered his food and was eating a little bit of it while standing by the counter not far from the register. My teenage co-workers were just talking to him and answering his questions matter-of-factly. Yet there was something about him that did not sit right with me. I had a sense of discernment that was so strong, that I just could not believe other people didn't have it. I was hoping that my co-workers would stop answering his questions. One question I distinctly remember him asking was whether we were busy on Sundays or not. He also asked them if we had a guard on Sundays. They did not think anything of it continuing to laugh, talk and act silly, but I felt that something was just not right, even though I was again, just sixteen.

A couple of weeks later, it was my night to handle the register. I took a short break to go to the restroom which was away from the counter area through the dining room and around a corner. As I entered the dining room to return to the register, I could see a man brandishing a gun at the girl taking my place at the register. He told her to give him the money out of the register and to sit on the floor and not to move. I tried my hardest to not attract his attention by sitting quietly down in the dining room. I felt that if I went back to the restroom, he would notice the movement.

One of my co-workers must have looked my way and that made him look at me. He pointed the gun at me and said "you, get over here and don't move or I will blow your brains out!" I eased my way over to the counter and I did exactly what he said. A gun was pointed at my head and I was bracing myself to die. In the meantime, someone was opening the safe to get the money out. As the thief left with the money, he warned us that if we called the police, he would come back and kill every one of us.

Well, that was my last night ever working there. I never worked at another fast food restaurant nor did I ever allow my own teenagers to work at one because of what I experienced that night.

When I reflected on the events of that night, I realized that the robbery had occurred on a Sunday, with no guard on staff and very few customers. The man who had questioned my co-workers was involved in setting us up. I believe that because it was my register that night, God had sent me to the restroom to relieve me from the register just before the man entered the restaurant to rob us. I would have been able to discern this man's spirit just as I had his partner and I could

have been killed or could have caused us all to be killed had I

reacted unfavorably. I am reminded of 1 Corinthians 2:12-16

> *"12 Now we have received, not the spirit of the world, but the spirit which is of God; that we might know the things that are freely given to us of God.13 Which things also we speak, not in the words which man's wisdom teacheth, but which the Holy Ghost teacheth; comparing spiritual things with spiritual. 14 But the natural man receiveth not the things of the Spirit of God: for they are foolishness unto him: neither can he know them, because they are spiritually discerned. 15 But he that is spiritual judgeth all things, yet he himself is judged of no man.16 For who hath known the mind of the Lord, that he may instruct him? but we have the mind of Christ."*

5

Life & Death

The angel of the lord encamps around those who fear him, and He delivers them. Psalm 34:7

Females between the ages of sixteen and twenty-five are possibly the most vulnerable demographic to abusive and violent crimes such as rape and murder, by the male species. As a high school teacher and first lady of a church, I have witnessed young ladies go from being vivacious, zealous and passionate young people with everything to live for, to being beaten down, emotionally distraught, feeling as if they have nothing to live for, because of mentally or emotionally abusive relationships, from the father, stepfather to their own boyfriend or their mother's boyfriend to their husbands.

The night sky has mesmerized me since I was a little girl. The whole neighborhood would be sound asleep and I would find myself looking out the window into the pleasantry of twinkling stars, rain clouds or mysterious full moon. I was comforted by nature itself. Even the pitter patter of raindrops found a special place in my heart.

Every set of buildings in the projects enclosed a parking lot for the residents. The lot served as a play-area for a game of tag, hide and go seek and of course hopscotch especially during the summer when we were just looking for the next adventure. When it rained ferociously, we called ourselves swimming in the dirty water that had accumulated along the border of the lot. The massive amount of kids living near each other meant that fun was the order of every given day. I was about seven or eight years old when my memory of the coveted parking lot would change.

Around two or three in the morning, I could not sleep so I drew the curtain back from the window to gaze at the dark sky. I noticed the movement of what appeared to be shadows. Our bedrooms were upstairs in the townhouse, so my attention was diverted from the heavenly sky to the activity taking place below. In in the middle of the parking lot was a raised partition, an island that divided the parked cars on the west from those on the east. The moving images were horizontal, and the sounds muffled. But there were two people in some sort of a scuffle. There were no bedroom lights flickering nor were there any streetlights shining down of the subjects. At some point, I went back to bed, confused but sleepy.

The mothers were young and high spirited. They would gather together to talk to each other while they braided their children's hair, swept the porch or smoked cigarettes. I remembered them talking about a "rake" had taken placed. I did not know what a "rake" was, but I could tell that whatever it was, it could not have been good.

Later, I would find out that "rake" was "rape" and that the tumultuous activity I had witnessed that night was indeed a woman being beaten and sexually assaulted on the same lot where my brothers held relay races and I played hop scotch and tag and dodge ball with my friends every day.

My high school students are required to write persuasive essays each year on social issue topics such as abortion, immigration, pollution and even domestic abuse. After conducting extensive research on emotional abuse, one young lady showed me her note cards and her interview responses. As we conferenced about her findings, her voice started to quiver. According to her research she was being emotionally abused by her father. Her mother was not in this country and she was forced to live with her father for reasons I did not know.

This young lady's dad would not speak to her unless it was to make her question her worth, her appearance or even her intelligence. He was not interested in her well-being from her grades to her health. He accused her of lying all the time, in fact she left her keys in my classroom accidentally on the last day of school and had to come back into the building to retrieve them. She had me call her father on his cell phone and tell him that she "really had left her keys" because if I had not told him, he would have beaten her for lying. The father held against his daughter whatever had transpired between himself and her mother. He was destroying the very core of his daughter's essence, grooming her for a life of self-doubt and relational distress.

Another young lady use to avoid my classroom all the time. She received an F on the first report card simply because she rarely came to class. At parent teacher conferences, I told her mother that she would tell me not to smile at her, that she hated me. She even said that she hated me at the conference. I told her in front of her mother, as often as I would tell her in the hallway that I loved her anyway. I told her that I knew that she could get an A if she just came to class. Of the couple assignments that she had completed, I knew that she was capable. She started coming reluctantly back to class so that she could hopefully pass my class and graduate on time. A young man she called her boyfriend came to my room while she was sitting at a desk and talking to me. There were only three of us in the room so it must have been my lunch hour. At some point during the conversation between the three of us, she picked up the heavy metal stapler that was on the desk and threw it at him. I blocked the stapler from hitting his head sustaining injuries to my hand instead. She had to be reprimanded by administration because I had been injured even though I was not the target, someone else was.

The Lord put it on my heart to tell her that she had deep rooted anger issues and that she really needed to talk to someone about them. I told her that I knew that something must have happened to her in her childhood and that she needed to release it, if not to me to a counselor or to another teacher. She looked at me side-eyed and asked, "how do you know?" I told her that the Lord told me.

The young lady finally revealed to me that her mother had lost a baby boy either during childbirth or right after. Her father blamed her mother, accusing her of not taking care of herself as well as she did with her pregnancy with my student. She said that her father looked at her with disgust, criticized her constantly and acted as if she did not exist. My eyes welled with tears. In all my years of teaching, I had never heard of such a wretched story. The mother was blamed for the miscarriage or still birth of her child, by her husband. The daughter was being rebuked because she lived, and the son had not. No wonder this girl despised the world! She could not accept the unconditional love that I had for her because she was in constant emotional abuse inflicted upon her by her own father. She did not even feel worthy of the smiles that I would give her.

I believe that my experience as a teenager in a controlling relationship with my boyfriend would drive me to be especially alert to emotionally abused women. I did not realize at the time that the relationship I was in was abusive. I had good solid parents who built a wonderful foundation for me and my siblings. Yet, I did not realize that a controlling and jealous boyfriend could be a deadly combination. There weren't many stories in the news about it or anything that I could remember.

My boyfriend at the time had a brand-new vehicle at the age of sixteen which was unheard of in the late 70's. "Nobody gets too much love anymore, it's as high as a mountain and harder to climb, you and me girl have a highway to the sky" by the Bee Gees or "Bad Girl" by Donna Summer would be blasting from his automobile announcing that he was indeed back in the neighborhood. I had been dating this guy for about three years, but since I lacked the knowledge that jealousy rules a controlling relationship and that love is not the author of intimidation, I was traveling through the forest without ever seeing the trees.

When a woman reveals that she was raped years after the incident, people tend to question her credibility. The humiliation that one feels when they are sexually assaulted is so traumatic to their psyche that even they don't want to believe that it happened. They rationalize with themselves, believing that they, the victim, played a part in the horrendous act. But they know without a shadow of a doubt that they did not want to be violated and that the trust they had in the person left them vulnerable.

In the early dusky evening of late July, my boyfriend

said that he was going to take me to a restaurant that was quite a drive from our neighborhood. As the streets started to narrow, the trees appeared to be taller, the sky less visible through the branches heavy laden with leaves and the houses and buildings slowly one by one, tiptoed away, my mind became suspect. We were in the thick of the woods. What was he planning to do? Why had we come here? Why were we so far from civilization? I was in high school and my only reason for having a boyfriend was because in my mind you had to have a boyfriend in high school. There was no other reason for me to be with this guy.

My boyfriend happened to see me walking down the street with another guy as he was driving home from his job. A day or so later, at my boyfriend's request, I walked the five or six houses down to his doorstep. I knew that he had seen me with the other young man, but we had not discussed it all. Upon my arrival at his door, his mother and eighteen-year old sister came running out of the house yelling to me that he was going to shoot me. Birds were chirping, kids were riding their bikes down the street and cars were zooming by. It happened in broad daylight. I stood there in disbelief and sure enough, he came out of the house with a gun, aiming it towards the sky, he pulled the trigger and shot the gun up in the air several times. He told me that if he ever saw me with the guy again that he would kill me and the guy. I did not disclose this information to my parents. I was too ashamed to tell them even though I had a great relationship with them. Some-kind of way, I found fault with myself. My teenage mind reasoned that I could handle this dilemma. I knew that I did not like this young man anymore and I decided that I would go out with him one more time to tell him that our relationship was over. He picked me up from my house to take me to dinner and to see a movie. I noticed that he was not saying much of anything and that he was looking straight ahead. We had not discussed where we would eat but he continued to drive. The Lord put in my spirit that he was going to try to kill me. He started driving in a direction that would not have led to anywhere we were used to going. His profile was deliberate and fixated on something in his head. My spirit was disturbed by the coldness emitting from his person, but I could not allow him to feel my apprehension. As he approached the downtown area, I could tell that he was heading for Belle Isle which is an island park in Detroit. The only way to get to it is via bridge or boat. The Detroit River is known for its treacherous current and many people have committed suicide from that bridge or been thrown from it.

I told the Lord that I would never ever allow myself to get in this type of situation again, if He would just spare my life. Sure enough, my boyfriend turned right onto the bridge exiting Jefferson Avenue. The night was still, the river was black and there were no cars behind us. We could barely see the tail lights of the car in front of us which meant that no one would see or hear us if he were to make his move. I was holding my breath, praying and asking God what to say to him. He told me to keep talking and not to mention that I was breaking up with him. I continued to make small talk and never once mentioned that I was breaking up with him. I prayed, I sat still and I listened to the Lord. Facing death, or the uncertainty of the outcome of a seemingly impossible situation is something that we will all do some day. Seeking, praising and serving the Lord when we are not in trouble, when we are not in a hard place, when we are not at our wits end will get us to a place in Him that we can rest comfortably, make requests and recognize His voice.

4 I sought the Lord, and he heard me, and delivered me from all my fears. 5 They looked unto him, and were lightened: and their faces were not ashamed. 6 This poor man cried, and the Lord heard him, and saved him out of all his troubles. 7 The angel of the Lord encampeth round about them that fear him, and delivereth them. 8 O taste and see that the Lord is good: blessed is the man that trusteth in him. Psalm 34:4-8. (KJV)

He drove around that three-mile island several times, as if looking for a point of final-destination for me. He could shoot me and toss me into the depths of that deep and dreadful river known for its undercurrent, or he could drive his car into the river with us both in it. I made light of being hungry, but I must have said something about the beautiful night as chills ran up and down my spine. I would not allow my voice to quiver, my eyes to let on that my spirit was not at rest. To do so could justify a conversation about that moment he saw me with the other guy inciting the rage that catapulted him to fire the shots in the air threatening my life just a few days prior. He turned down a dirt road onto a path that lacked any evidence of light, through thick trees laden with the sounds of night creatures. He could snap my neck and throw me into the woods. The animals would devour me before anyone could find my mangled body. I was at his mercy, so he thought. I continued to pray silently, only saying a word or two here and there, that I could think of that would not set off an alarm that I knew what he was up to. There was a battle going on in his head. He eventually drove out of the thickness, back onto the main road, completed the circle and approached the bridge. As he made his way down the lodge freeway, I thanked God, giving Him praise for ordering my steps.

When I got out of the car, he did not open the door for me as I had become accustomed to, nor did he look my way. He stared straight ahead, his assignment to end my life abruptly cancelled by the most-high God. He pulled off towards his house, which a couple of years later would become a major crime scene.

I was away at college and free from that unhealthy relationship. My ex-friend's father had a car accident of which he was found with a woman that was not his wife. His wife left him upon discovering her husband's affair. He told her that if she ever came back home that he would kill her.

One summer morning, I was home from college. I happened to be in my parent's room. Looking out of their window, I noticed that the father of my ex-friend was driving down the street in his work van at a time much different than the norm in that he was an extremely early riser and it had to be close to ten am. An uneasy feeling came over me. Moments later, emergency sirens were screaming down our shady once well-behaved, manicured street. Our neighbors ran outside with their robes on, holding their breath, hands over their mouths, calming their pets as the news began to break that death had found its way to our doors.

The mother of my ex-friend had come back home some months later, after having left the father, to pick up some articles of clothing. She had taken up residence with a dear friend of hers. He, enraged that she had the audacity to leave him even though he cheated on her, emptied his pistol on her as well as their daughter who was slated to graduate from high school that year. The most horrific sound I had ever heard at that time was the youngest child returning home from a relative to find out that her mother and big sister had been brutally murdered by her father.

When the father turned himself in hours later, the police were aware that he had killed his wife because she left him, but they asked what had motivated him to kill his eighteen-year-old daughter. He replied that he had no recollection of killing his daughter.

The last date with my high school boyfriend could have been the last day of my life. Had I not recognized God's voice and allowed my words to utter fear or contempt, I knew without the shadow of a doubt that when I was with him in that car on that day that I would have been killed just as unfortunately his mother and sister had been. I am a living testimony that God is constantly speaking to His children. He

will tell you not to walk down a certain street, what to say on

a job interview, when to switch lanes and how to keep

someone from committing suicide.

> ⁹ *Because thou hast made the Lord, which is my refuge,*
> *even the most, High thy habitation;* ¹⁰ *There shall no evil befall thee,*
> *neither shall any plague come nigh thy dwelling.* ¹¹ *For he shall give*
> *his angels charge over thee, to keep thee in all thy ways.*¹² *They shall*
> *bear thee up in their hands, lest thou dash thy foot against a*
> *stone.*¹³ *Thou shalt tread upon the lion and adder: the young lion and*
> *the dragon shalt thou trample under feet. Psalm 91:9-13.*

Question: How will I know that what I am hearing is the voice of God?

Wise Actions	I. Pray with supplication and thanksgiving
	II. Read your bible, start with Proverbs
	III. Lean not onto your own understanding
	IV. Be obedient in all things
	V. Ask for forgiveness
	VI. Forgive others
Wisdom Words	As you do these things you build a relationship with God.

6

The Stranger

Though I walk in the midst-of trouble, thou wilt revive me: thou shalt stretch forth thine hand against the wrath of mine enemies, and thy right hand shall save me. Psalm 138:7

I would attend Eastern Michigan University upon graduation from high school. My best friend Wendy and I were set to be roommates. We bought matching blue comforters, sheets and bean bag chairs. My parents bought the microwave, her parents the refrigerator. I brought an iron and she the ironing board. We favored in appearance and people just assumed that we were related but we were not.

There was a young lady who ran a game called the "numbers." You would place a bet in hopes of winning the cash prize. She just took your money and forwarded it to someone in Detroit. If you won, there was a payoff waiting for you. This day, I decided that I would play a three-digit number. I came up with the number of my mother's license plate which was 162. I did not know anything about gambling, or the sin factor associated with it, but I knew that I wanted to play 162. Later that evening, I met my best friend at the campus library, and I asked her to choose a number that she thought might win. She picked 162 as well. The number 162 fell that evening and my little 19-year-old self, won $250 dollars which was like a thousand dollars to a teen in the 1980's.

From that point on, I tried to figure what the winning numbers would be for the night. I played the numbers until I ran out of money trying to play them. I eventually lost a semester of school because I could not concentrate on classes for trying to figure out the next winning number. I found out the hard way why gambling is a sin. You can become addicted and lose sight of what it is that really matters, which was at the time, my education.

However, knowing that I was "going to win" feeling would happen every so often. It could be a school raffle as it was twice. I told my co-worker that I was going to win. When I won the first time, she was shocked. We were in computer training session and I told her that I was going to win the t-shirt raffle, because I knew that I was going to win. She said to me, well you said it before and you won, but this is the second time. Unbelievable!

I walked into a store to get a bottle of water. I was somewhere on the east side. It was hot outside and I just wanted some water and to sit down somewhere cool while I drank the water. There was a raffle going on in one of the departments, so I entered my name. I told a lady who had also entered the raffle that I was going to win. I just knew that I was. When the man called my name, she looked at me and thought that the game was rigged. I had never been to the store before in my life and had never met the man. It is just that when I know something. I just know.

My husband and I were visiting with his mother as we had done weekly on Sundays for many years. As we were leaving this particular evening through the garage, "fire hazard" entered my mind. I had seen that garage thousands of times over the last twenty-five years, but this evening, fire hazard came to my mind and I mentioned it to my husband.

The next day my husband was at his mother's house and the smoke alarm went off in the house. There was no apparent fire in the house, so they just ignored the alarm. When he got ready to leave, the doorknob to the garage was hot and there was indeed a fire taking place in the garage.

My life is riddled with incidents of knowing without a doubt about something. I cannot predict a thing. But, when I feel strongly about something, it is inevitable.

There was a girl that I attended parochial school with from 1st to 8th grade, who I had not seen since our graduation. I was in my late thirties by this time. Her name was Diane M. I won't mention her last name, but she attended St. Christopher Catholic School in Detroit in the late sixties, early seventies. Her name came across my mind so many times this day that it was unnerving.

There was a popular strip mall called Tel=Twelve in the city of Southfield, years ago that I would frequent from time to time. I had to make a stop there to pick something up this hot summer day. Of all the people that I know in this city and this county, who would I run into? None other than Diane M. who I had not seen in twenty-five years. It was so incredibly unbelievable, but I was starting to get use to the extraordinary and the unbelievable, happening to me.

A young man by the name of Charles that I did not have the slightest interest in told me that one day I would be his wife. I told him that he did not know me and that he was just infatuated with me, but I felt a very strange connection to him. Well, four years of his pursuing me led me to believe that he indeed was serious. He started walking with me to a church near campus. We eventually fell in love and committed ourselves to each other through marriage. The Lord blessed us with four children.

We rented a townhouse the first few years of our marriage. Every time we had a child, we had to find another place to rent. Eventually, the Lord lead us to what would become our first home. The house was nestled in a very well-manicured, two parent, two income, family-oriented suburb called Southfield. Most of our neighbors were engineers, teachers, business owners or professionals of some kind. We hadn't had a lot of issues with criminal activity such as robbery, rapes or home invasions, so most residents felt a sense of neighborhood security.

One fluffy winter night, I found myself looking in the classified ads of the newspaper. It could have been the snow glistening outside my window, or the cup of hot chocolate I was sipping, that lead me to feel the need for another baby, or puppy, I should say. I noticed that someone was selling newborn Akita's. I knew that an Akita was a mix between an Alaskan Husky and a Malamute and that they were beautiful dogs. I mentioned to my husband that our children had really expressed interest in owning a dog. I pictured them being pulled by this beautiful dog in the snow having the time of their lives.

As Christmas approached, I was able to convince my husband to get the kids a dog. We went to see the Akita breeder and there were only two puppies left. The one we fell in love with had sandy brown fur and it was adorable. We named her Honey. The kids loved her of course, but not too long after they got her, they stopped feeding her or cleaning up behind her.

One cold January evening around eleven maybe even twelve o'clock midnight, the kids were up playing with their Christmas presents still on vacation from school. It was time for Honey to take a quick walk. Normally, I would shut the front door and walk Honey to the corner of the street which was a few houses down. My father had bought me a pepper spray gadget that I could spray into someone's eyes as a self-defense mechanism if ever necessary. The evening was quiet, lacking emotion but I reluctantly put the spray into my pocket. I had not read the directions as how to use it, but I put it in my pocket anyway. Also, I left the door open with the light on in the foyer. I had not done this on any occasion before, even though I walked the dog every night.

Our walkway was quite long and even though the foyer light was on, a person walking down the street would not necessarily see the light if he hadn't been looking towards the house. We did not have a sidewalk in front of our house, so I literally was walking in the street with our dog Honey. As I was walking, this eerie feeling came over me, like none that I had known before. The puppy was still so little that she hadn't given me any kind of warning that someone was approaching, or maybe she couldn't smell or hear because of the amount of snow that was on the ground, whatever the reason, Honey, gave me no indication that a stranger was approaching me from behind. I had not heard a thing; I just had this overwhelming feeling that I was in danger. I grabbed hold to the pepper spray in my pocket and realized that I could not use it. As I turned around this man of about six feet five or so dressed in a face mask, army fatigues and dark heavy boots, was walking towards me in somewhat of a purposeful gait, swinging his long arms and stepping in a way that was deliberate and intimidating. My immediate neighbors were senior citizens so even if I ran towards their house, he could snap my neck before they ever reached the door. As I looked at him the Lord told me to look at the door to my house. When I looked at the door to my house, he looked at the door too. He could see the foyer light on and the door ajar. Had I not yielded to the voice in me that said turn around now, that I would have been raped and/or murdered that night.

I was telling my husband what happened to me and not long after that, we saw lights from police cars flashing on our street. Our house was on the corner, and directly across the street at another neighbor's house were the police. I called my neighbor after the police left and she told me that she had called the police because she had seen a man looking at her through her front window. The same man was the man that was approaching me from the direction of her house.

First of all, before I ever went outside, God was warning me not to go otherwise I would not have felt the need to grab the pepper spray or to leave the door open and the foyer light on, again this was something that I had never done before. So, deep down I knew that I should not be going out that night, but I did it anyway.

God showed me that night, that not only must I listen and obey His voice, that even when I think something like pepper spray can protect me, I need to be always looking to Him for His direction. The pepper spray did not work, and the dog did not bark. But I turned around just as He told me to and faced my potential attacker. I looked at my front door when He told me to and the man looked at my front door, saw the light (in more ways than one) and proceeded down the street.

The voice of God is real. When we are on bended knee praying for protection, praying for healing or direction, He hears us and places His heavenly angels around us. For us to recognize His voice, we must have, a relationship with Him.

Later, that week, I found out that there had recently been a series of rapes reported in a business parking structure located less than a mile from my home. I believe my ability to discern the spirit of this man, before I ever saw him is what kept me from being raped and possibly losing my life that night.

Seek the things of God.
Sing praises to His name.
Obey His commandments.
Honor His Life.

7

UNEXPECTED GUEST

²⁰ Bless the LORD, ye his angels, that excel in strength, that do his commandments, hearkening unto the voice of his word. Psalm 103:20

I have never seen a movie that I did not like where a train ride was the major setting. Why the orchestrated curving and gliding of a traveling train provides the same tranquility to me as resting under a Weeping Willow on a breezy summer evening does, I cannot say. Even more so, the country-side mom and pop shops, the dated ticket stations and the stony streams just propel my mind to a place of peace and clear thinking about nothing but the uniqueness and beauty of it all.

I was traveling on a train from Michigan to Los Angeles with my youngest daughter to visit my best friend and her daughters. The route would take about 48 hours. I brought the book "Purpose Driven Life" with me to read on the way. At the time, I was not aware that it was to be read over time, not in one sitting. I would make my way to the observation car to read the book while soaking in the view. My purpose for being on that train would slowly be revealed to me. On a trip to the concession car to grab something to drink, one of the attendants started a conversation with me. He may have asked me if I was happily married or something along that line. He ended up telling me that his girlfriend left taking everything that he owned. He emphasized that she had even taken a bible that a family member had left to him. He could not figure out why she took the bible, knowing that it meant so much to him. Because he was talking about the bible, I knew that the Lord had placed me there at that moment in time to give him closure about that bible. I said to him "she took the bible because she needed it at that time in her life more than you did. That she made the decision to leave the relationship, had to have been one of the hardest things that she had ever done, and she knew that having that bible in her possession would give her the strength to move forward.

He told me that he had never thought of it like that. His countenance changed and I knew that I had fulfilled my purpose for being at that concession stand at that moment.

Later in the journey, I was in the observation car. I may have been reading but at some point, I was just looking out of the window admiring the tranquility of the golden hues of the sunset before me. No one else was in the observation car at the time. A young man of about eighteen years of age and of a different race, came and sat kitty corner to me. Our knees almost touched. I don't know how the conversation started but I recall his telling me that he was from New York and that he was atheist. Right away, I thought to myself "ok Lord, I see what you are doing, just help me."

The young man shared with me that his parents were atheist and that he really had not had a favorable upbringing. I asked him if he had ever read any of the bible. He responded that he had no reason to do so. I said to him that he owed it to himself to at least give the bible a chance. I asked him how he could be satisfied with a directive from parents who had not done right by him in the first place.

The Lord made it very clear to me that this train ride coupled with the premise of the book "Purpose Driven Life" was taking me to a level of understanding that would hold me accountable for my "witness" for the rest of my life. There are no coincidences in this journey that we are taking with the Lord. We only have one lifetime to get it right.

Be not forgetful to entertain strangers: for thereby some have entertained angels unaware. Hebrews 13:2 KJV

8

The Fire

He answered and said, Lo, I see four men loose, walking in the midst of the fire, and they have no hurt; and the form of the fourth is like the son of God. Daniel 3:25-28

My husband and I decided to put our first home up for sale in 2001 and to start procedures to build our next home. Our children were fifteen, fourteen, twelve and ten years old at the time. My husband had been holding bible studies for about four years on a weekly basis by that time in a cafeteria of a school. He was not a pastor yet, but we had left our first church which was pastored by his uncle and had become members of a much larger church which was pastored by his cousin who was a highly acclaimed pastor from a very well-known Christian family.

Our two sons and two daughters were scholars and serious athletes. I owned a tutoring business in the neighborhood, and my husband coached basketball, football, baseball and he had even started the city's first community track team. By trade my husband was an engineer and I, a teacher. We were one of the most well-known families in the city at that time.

September 28th, 2001 would be a day that my family and I would never forget. My husband held his bible study the night before as usual. This evening, he replayed a movie he had shown earlier in his ministry, about a man who was severely burned as a result of a household fire in which the furnace or a gas leak of some kind had caused his house to explode. While I can't remember the details of the movie, I recall that the man was a man of great faith and that his story moved my husband because the fact, that he survived, was nothing short of a miracle.

The morning of September 28th, 2001 was a particularly stressful morning for me, because I had gotten up early to wash my hair. I hadn't had time the night before because of the busy schedule of bible study, after school sports, cooking and anything else that you could think of having a house full of active teens, two working parents and a minister and business owner to name a few. I washed my hair not knowing that my hair dryer was broken. I teach high school students, so there was no way I could go to work looking any old kind of way, because my students would not be able to get pass my hair.

I soon realized that I was running late for work. The one thing I hated to do was to be late for work. It would happen from time to time but it really made me feel horrible because I did not like to do that to my students. Even though my tardiness was never because I had overslept, but just simply because of the ordeal of having a tough time getting four kids off to school. By that time my kids were attending three different schools. My husband left very early for work leaving the "get the kids ready in a hurry" issues all on me. Earlier that week, I had told myself that if I was ever late again, I would find another job closer to home. I had even asked my daughter if they were hiring at her high school. All of this would be brought back to me much later.

People were still numb from the tragic events of September 11th, 2001, which had just occurred a little over two weeks prior to this day. I went to work, hair wet and all, disgusted because I was late. I had an ordinary day at work, but I still felt defeated because of that tumultuous morning and I knew that I could not go on like that, rushing around and exhausted.

My neighbor called and told me that her church was having youth night. She said that there would be all kinds of character-building activities for the kids to do as well as food. I promised God that I would make my children go to the youth night. They had been so involved in their sports and other activities that they hadn't participated in Christian related activities since we had left the other church. Because we had not officially joined the new church, our kids could not participate in any type of youth activities and I was determined to make them participate in this one.

When my husband and sons returned from football practice, I told them that I wanted them to go to this youth event at our neighbor's church. My husband and my sons made all kinds of excuses as to why they could not go, and I reluctantly gave in. Forgetting the promise that I had made to God, that I was going to make them go no matter what, I gave in to the pressure of my husband and my sons and allowed them to stay home.

I started making hamburgers and French fries when my oldest son called me into the family room which was around the corner from the kitchen. A parent wanted to speak with me regarding her daughter attending homecoming with my son. He said that she just had a question about the limousine and the events that would take place the night of the homecoming. What was supposed to be a quick response to a question ended up being a ten-minute conversation. I returned to the kitchen to find the cooking oil in flames within the pot. I had forgotten that I was cooking.

I immediately had my children and their friends evacuate the house. My husband came running down the stairs as I warned him to leave with me. He thought he could put the fire out, after all, the flames were contained within a pot. My kids and I were screaming from outside the kitchen window for him to leave the house, to get out of the kitchen. We could see the intensity of the flames and we knew that something terrible was bound to happen if my husband stayed in the house.

My neighbor was calling me from her house for me to give her my address, she had the emergency people on the line, as I turned to go towards her house, I heard what sounded like an explosion. When I looked back at the house, I could see that the upstairs bedroom light was on and that assured me that my husband was still alive. I reached the neighbor's house to give the address. As I came back across the street someone was motioning my husband who had managed to get out of the house, to get in the car to go to the hospital. Out of the turmoil, appeared my twelve-year-old son Sidney, his face burned black. I went into shock. He was not in the house; how could he have been burned? As the lady attempted to get my son and husband in her car, the ambulances arrived.

They put my son in one vehicle and my husband in another. Everything appeared to be playing out in slow motion, from the fire trucks, to the people who had gathered, to the men working on my husband and son. How could my son be burned? He was not in the house? I would not find out until days later that my youngest son had tried to go back into the house, just as my husband was trying to throw the pot of grease and flames out of the same door. If my husband had not dropped the pot and fallen into the flames on the ceramic tile, he would have thrown the flame filled grease into my son who was trying to go into the house to save him. Instead, my son's clothes caught on fire. My other son saw him running, clothes on fire and immediately reacted by throwing him down on the ground and making him roll.

There are no words that can describe the devastation my family experienced that night. For two weeks, I walked from Children's Hospital to Detroit Receiving hospital through a tunnel that connected the hospitals. The events were playing themselves out before me and it appeared that they were not going to stop. The movie I was watching was the story of me. I just kept praying "Lord just give me the strength; Lord please just give me the strength that I need to be here for my family."

My husband suffered 3rd degree burns over 33 percent of his body. My youngest son suffered 3rd degree burns on his head, face and shoulder. It would take several surgeries and much prayer to get them back to looking like their normal selves. But that is just how good God is!

Had I followed my first mind and taken the kids to the

youth program that night instead of giving in to the pressure to allow them to stay home, would all of this have happened? I will never know.

My son only weighed 98 pounds at the time of the accident. I knew that the burns were bad, but I just figured ok, burns can heal. What I did not realize is that infection could set in and cause serious problems. After the doctors shaved his hair, they wrapped my son's head with white bandages. He looked like a mummy, something out of a horror movie. The only thing you could see were his eyes, barely his nose and mouth. My son's head swelled to the size of a bowling ball. His head was so heavy that I could not lift his head to lay it comfortably on the pillow.

Once the swelling went down, they would shave his head daily. He could not have even one strand of hair on his head because hair was considered filthy in that it caught all kinds of germs and bacteria. They would then place my son in a silver aluminum tub and proceed to bathe him and nurture his wounds. In the meantime, I would go through the twilight zone tunnel, I called it, to feed my husband his breakfast. His arms and legs were bandaged. Even though his face was burned, by the time he left the hospital, there were no signs of the burns to his face. My husband was so sedated that until this day, he does not remember certain conversations or events that took place during the time he was in the hospital and the first weeks he returned to his mother's house, which was where we stayed while our house was being repaired.

One conversation my husband and I had was of course the conversation of why? He wondered how this could happen to him when he was doing everything that he knew to serve God. He had taught bible study the night before. He had re-shown a movie about a man miraculously surviving a house explosion just a week prior to this accident. But why had this happened to him?

The test we often find ourselves in is to show us who we really are in Christ Jesus, because whether we believe it or not, He already knows. He knows how we are going to respond; He knows how or if we will continue to walk with Him. He knows if we will give a testimony so that someone else may see the light.

There is a television series out now about true survival stories, stories that if you haven't lived through something like that it would be hard to believe that someone could. I believe that the people that are spared their lives are the ones who are given a second chance to either get it right, or to be a living testimony of God's miraculous power to those that are still here. I believe that there is always a spiritual reason why people are spared their lives in the most catastrophically unheard of, events.

During the two weeks my husband and son were in the hospital, they only got to see each other once. My husband never witnessed his son looking like a skeleton with his head swollen the size of a bowling ball, nor did he see him going through the excruciating pain of bandage changing and body shavings. My son did not see his dad's limbs suspended in air nor did he witness the humiliation his dad felt when he could not lift his own fork to feed himself or reach his straw to sip his juice. He did not know that his dad could not even brush his own teeth.

Between Children's hospital and Detroit Receiving there was this astonishment at the visitors check in desk because of the hundreds of people who came to visit the two of them that week or that came to offer me their support. Again, my husband coached just about every sport available in Southfield. Not only did he teach his own bible study class, but we were also members of a very large congregation at the time. Our children played just about every sport, they were academic scholars and even though I taught in Detroit at the time, I owned a tutoring business in the Southfield which catered to hundreds of the city's residents. So, the hospital employees admitted to being blown away by the number of people that came to the hospital during-the-course of the two weeks.

One visitor, a friend of my husband, but also a teacher, revealed to me that he had just been hired to teach in Southfield. He let me know that there were some openings at the high school level and that I should apply. At the time, looking at the condition of my husband and my son, work was the last thing on my mind. In fact, because of the severity of their burns, I did not see myself ever working again. So, his words went in one ear and out of the other. My husband, however, was paying attention and he told me that I was going to have to go back to work one day, and that I should go ahead and apply for the position.

Applicants had to apply online. The one thing that was left at my home was the computer. When you have a fire that does not burn the house down, a restoration team comes and takes everything out, because of the smoke. There was not even a belt buckle left in that house. The one thing that I told the restoration team to do was to keep the computer there in case the kids needed it. I drove to the house that Sunday evening by myself. I had not been there since the night of the fire. I had been spending the night at the hospital, taking breaks only to run errands while family members or friends stayed with my husband and son.

I had not slept in a bed since the fire, which had been about a week because I was always at the hospital. I remember clutching the wheel so extremely tightly, just praying that I would not have a car accident. I felt as if someone was deliberately pressing down my eyelids because I was so sleep deprived.

When I opened the front door of my house, the smoke-filled emptiness of the edifice took me aback. Prior to the fire, we had renovated the house to sell it. We were in the process of having another house built. The ominous smoke-filled dwelling brought on a sudden overwhelming feeling of painful regret to me. But even in that painful instant where the events of that night flashed before my eyes, God was reassuring me that my family and I would be alright.

In order to apply for the high school teaching position, I had to go to the back of the house to use the computer. They had taken the lamp out of the family room, so the only light in the room was the light from the desktop computer. I had to kneel on the floor to type because there was not even a chair left in the house. I knew that I was supposed to be doing this at this time. I just knew it. The Lord would confirm it very quickly.

Your ears will hear a word behind you, "This is the way, walk in it," whenever you turn to the right or to the left. Isaiah 30:21

9
The Job

[132] *Look thou upon me, and be merciful unto me, as thou use to do unto those that love thy name.* [133] *Order my steps in thy word: and let not any iniquity have dominion over me. Psalm 119:132-133*

I figured that there would only be a couple of pages to the application from the school and that I would be able to head back to the hospital within an hour or so. The application was eight pages long. Each question required a short essay response. I remember praying and asking God to please help me respond correctly because I was falling asleep. At the time, the school district I was applying to, was one of the hardest districts to get into because the perks were excellent, and the pay was higher than most of the districts in the Michigan. Even though I had no desire to leave where I was, except for the fact that the drive was long, I just obeyed my husband and completed the application.

I don't even remember driving back to the hospital because of the daze I was in. I get chills when I think of all the miracles that took place during that time period.

Monday morning, my mother-in-law got a call from the district requesting for me to call the human resource center. I had just completed the application that Sunday night and they were already calling me! I called them back and of course they set up an interview with me. I did not even have clothes to go on the interview. My mother in-law who was two sizes larger than I was, found a black skirt in her closet for me to wear that happened to be my size... I had a blazer in my trunk that I had recently picked up from the cleaners. The school had been without an English teacher since August. My daughter, who was a senior at the time, had been telling me that they were short teachers, but because I liked everything about my current school except the distance, I had not applied. But the Lord brought back to my memory that the morning of the fire,

I had said if I was ever late again, that I would look for another job closer to my house.

Anyway, the interview was Tuesday. I still had not had any sleep. The principal of the school, the English department head and the reading specialist were throwing questions at me from all over the place. I don't remember what I said, or how I had the strength to say it. I left everything in God's hands.

I was offered the position the next day which was a Wednesday. The principal invited me to meet the teachers at a parent teacher's conference on that Thursday because the teachers would be in the gymnasium for the conferences. I remember him taking me around to meet the teachers.

Remember, I had not been to sleep but a couple hours in a chair here and there in by now the last two weeks. The first forty-eight hours my son was in the hospital he could not eat or drink. So, because he could not eat or drink, I did not eat or drink. My weight was down, I was sleep deprived and yet, I was driving, interviewing for a teaching position that miraculously came out of nowhere.

I had to complete paperwork at the human resource building the following Monday, before I could start working. I ended up telling the human resource people about the fire and how my husband and son was burned. I shared with them that God had spared their lives and that He was helping me keep my sanity. I told them how I had heard that the district needed teachers because my daughter was a senior at the high school, but, I was not looking to leave my current position. As a matter of fact, based on the condition of my son and husband, work was the last thing on my mind. God literally was ordering my steps.

The human resource manager disclosed the salary I would get. The amount was about $7500 less than what I was making, which was a shock to me. I had always been told that the district paid more. I spoke to my husband and family members. They said it was up to me. I knew that I would need clarity from the Lord because it would be extremely difficult for me to take a pay cut. One of our daughters was about to go to college, so our expenses were about to soar.

If anything, I needed more money. I had a little talk with Jesus, and He assured me to go ahead and sign the contract. When I returned that Friday to sign the contract, the ladies in human resources were shouting Praise the Lord Darcel! You will be making $15,000 more than what you are currently making. Not only did God give me double what I thought I was going to have to give up, but my job was going to be less than ten minutes away!

Matthew reminds us in 6:33 *But seek ye first the kingdom of God, and his righteousness; and all these things shall be added unto you.*

My son had to be home-schooled for about six months following the fire. He would have several surgeries to re-construct facial scars and his scalp over the next couple of years. My husband had to have help going to the restroom, bathing and eating for several months. He would also have to endure several surgeries over the next year.

Within months of the fire, my oldest son, broke one of his fingers playing football. My hair fell out in one night from what appeared to be tainted shampoo. Imagine having to try to teach a bunch of teenagers the next day, practically bald. But, in the midst-of-it-all, I kept praising God and thanking Him for being who He is.

My mother in law was easily able to house the six of us while our home was being repaired. As quickly as the repairs were done the house sold. God had made it so that my daughter was accepted to the first University to which she applied and the one she really wanted to attend. Most of all, my husband and my son were recovering from serious injuries.

Would the tragic events of September 28th, 2001 have taken place had I had kept my promise to God that night to make my children attend a youth night at a neighbor's church? I will never know. But what I do know is that all things work together for the good to those who are in Christ Jesus. The son that was burned graduated from 8th grade with honors, and he would eventually receive a full athletic scholarship from Northwestern University in Evanston Illinois to play football. His face healed miraculously with little evidence of the burns he endured that night. He has since published a book "Fate of the Seed" and has a wife and a son. The oldest son who was hit by a car while riding his bike across a driveway in the fourth grade and ended up with a discrepancy of ¾ of an inch in leg length as a result of breaking his leg, and who also broke his finger, playing high school football would obtain a full scholarship to the University of Michigan to play football. He is an entrepreneur in sports entertainment. Our oldest daughter who was going through her senior year of high school, who I could not assist at all in the college process because of the tragic events that had taken place, was blessed to be accepted to Michigan State University at an onsite admission just weeks after the fire, is now a wife, a mother and an elementary school teacher with a Master's degree in technology. The youngest child of the four, who had to switch schools, leaving the friends she had grown to love over the years in a day's notice, is now a Packaging Engineer and gifted and well sought out owner of Prim Heiress Luxury Weddings and Events.

My husband, who was so severely burned that night, stopped teaching bible study for three years. He went back to his engineering position at GM a few months later, praying that God would continue to lead and guide him. He would start teaching bible study renting out classrooms in school buildings for the next two years. He accepted the call to Pastor in September of 2006 and within two and a half years of pastoring would be able to purchase a beautiful church edifice for his growing congregation.

I let my tutoring service go but was able to bless another tutoring business that was starting in the building, with my clients and so many referrals that they had to add additional office space.

God gave me a classroom within the library of my new school. It was tucked away from the traffic of the high school drama filled hallways. My administrators had no idea that I was functioning on less than two hours of sleep a night. They did not know that practically every other moment I was just praying "God please help me stay awake, Please, give me the strength to make it through this day." My son's face was so badly burned and stripped of color, that he was ashamed for anyone other than myself to change his bandages which had to be changed every few hours. My husband couldn't eat or drink or bathe himself without assistance. So, even though my mother-in-law was cooking for us and helping as much as she could, most of the work was on me. My parents lived quite a distance away but would assist me in taking the other children to their different practices and activities.

I had to make most of the decisions about the house that was being renovated and sold. When you are building a house, you decide on everything from the kind of roof you want, to the kind of bricks you want to the kind of doorknobs you want. On top of that I had to write lesson plans and grade hundreds of high school essays and papers on less than two hours of sleep a night! Nothing but the blood of Jesus could sustain me. I get chills just thinking about what the Lord has brought me and my family through.

"Cast thy burden upon the LORD, and he shall sustain thee: he shall never suffer the righteous to be moved." Psalm 55:22

10

The Vision

My oldest daughter was a student at Michigan State University at the time of this next incident. The insurance on my vehicle had recently lapsed but I knew that I had to make the hour-long trip to her school that evening after work. I had a conversation with my aunt that morning. I told her that I had to go to MSU that day as I had done on very many occasions. But for some reason, I kept having visions of a deer sliding across the highway in front of my vehicle. The feeling was so overwhelming, that as I was driving toward Lansing, Michigan I was gripping the steering wheel as to brace myself for the deer that was to come.

I made it to my daughter's apartment in one piece. I

still had to make the journey home, but the deer was no longer an issue because it was dark outside, and they were known to pop out during dusk or dawn. I just prayed that God would protect me as I drove insurance-less in the pouring rain sixty miles per hour. About thirty minutes in to the drive, as I was shifting from the fast lane to the middle lane, the SUV that had been behind me sped up and just as I got over into the other lane a deer jumped over the median the SUV hit the deer and the deer slid across the front of my car head facing me eyes black as tar, just I had seen it happen in the vision hours prior. It was as if I had seen a ghost. But in fact, it was the Holy Ghost showing me once again, that His voice is real.

I could have lost control of my vehicle because I was screaming and hyperventilating, not out of fear, but because it was the vision I had seen over and over in my head that day. If I had not obeyed God's order to switch lanes the second that I did, my vehicle would have hit the deer. I could have died or possibly caused the death of someone else, but had I lived my uninsured vehicle would have been destroyed.

Either way, God had been preparing me that I would see a

deer slide to his death in front of my moving vehicle on that

day.

11

SCHOLARSHIP

⁸ But if I were you, I would appeal to God; I would lay my cause before him.⁹ He performs wonders that cannot be fathomed, miracles that cannot be counted. ¹⁰ He provides rain for the earth; he sends water on the countryside. Job 5:8-10

My youngest child of four was attending an out of state university for her first two years of college. Weeks prior to this day, I had applied for a loan to help pay her second semester tuition. I had also applied for a scholarship through the university. The loan was denied, and I never heard another thing about that scholarship. It was just a few days before my daughter was to fly back from Michigan to Tennessee to start the new semester. Of all the children, this child would have been the most devastated if she could not return to college, but I had absolutely no money to send her back.

My husband paid all the household bills and I was responsible for the college tuition for my daughters. Thank

God, my two sons were able to secure full athletic scholarships to play football, because my husband and I had not managed to save enough money to send any of them to college. In fact, I was still paying on my college loans.

I did not want my daughter, who already had her bags packed to go back to school, to worry about returning, but I had to tell her that I just did not have the money and I had nowhere to get it. She said to me, "My bags are packed Mom and I am getting on the plane in a couple days to go back to Tennessee." What she did not understand at the time was that she would eventually be kicked out of the dorm and she would not even be able to eat on campus because there was absolutely no money. I was on my prep period at work and I remember wondering how on earth I could tell this child who had worked harder than any child I know, on everything, from grades to organizations, to sports, that she could not go back to school. I had not had to face this dilemma with the other three children.

I remember feeling as though I had failed my daughter miserably. My heart sank to such a low that it is bringing tears to my eyes as I regurgitate the emotions I felt at that time. Here I was, teaching other high school students that there is nothing that they could not do if they just put their minds to it, and I had failed to save or secure the funds to keep my own daughter in college. I walked downstairs to the girls' restroom in tears. I was hoping that there wouldn't be any students in the restroom that could witness my pain.

I asked God, how to tell my daughter that she could not go back to school. I begged him to give me an answer because I knew how devastating the news was going to be to her. In the brokenness of that moment, a sudden peace came over me, He said to me as I struggled to keep the tears from trickling down my face in case a student came in the restroom, *"As I was with Moses, so I will be with you; I will never leave you nor forsake you. (Joshua 1:5).* The comfort in His voice assured me that everything would be ok.

As I entered my classroom the phone rang. It was the school secretary telling me that my daughter was on the phone and that she had been trying to reach me. She asked me if I had checked her school account lately. I told her that I had been checking her account all day because the payment was due today, otherwise her classes would be dropped and that she would not be able to return to the university. I let her know that I had done everything that I knew to do. I had even tried to take retirement funds out weeks prior to no avail.

My daughter said that she was checking on her account and that it looked as if she had a zero balance. I remember thinking, "Wow, Lord, I did not ask you for the money, I just asked you how to tell her that I did not have the money. But You knew what I had need of even though I could not utter the words."

My students were about to come into the room. So, I said with calmness, ok, but double check with your financial aid department, because I have been checking your account all day, and that is not what I see. But deep down inside I knew that God had made a way. I told her to call me after she had gotten a chance to go over to the financial aid office to make sure.

So, later that evening my husband and I and the board members of our fairly new congregation were to go look at a potential church building because we had been holding service out of a local university's auditorium since we started the church, which had been about two years. We were walking through the church and we all new at once that this was going to be our new home. We walked through the aisles praying over the pews the floors the walls, everything. The original goal was to buy a building by our fifth year of existence, and we were only into our second year and this beautiful edifice was about to become our very own.

As we were leaving the building, my daughter called me and said to me "Mom, there was no mistake, my tuition and room and board is paid for this semester." I started screaming and thanking God! My husband and the board members were praising God with me. I went back to earlier that day and that moment in the girl's restroom, when I was at the lowest point of my life. To tell your child that she can't go to finish her education and your parents who weren't educated saw to it that you were able to, was a tremendous weight that was killing me inside. God whispered into my being that He would never leave me nor forsake me and that He had always had my back.

So, later it dawned on me that I had applied for a scholarship, and that the Lord had blessed her with the scholarship that I had applied for, for her. I called to inquire about it being a renewable scholarship some months later, assuming the Lord had blessed her with the scholarship that I had originally applied for. The financial aid department told me that the scholarship she had been awarded had absolutely nothing to do with the one that I applied for. The University had just given her a full scholarship for that semester out of the blue. I knew that it was nothing but God, because her classes would have dropped at midnight that night if the money had not come through.

Because we are human, we will have times where we feel that we are up against the wall, especially when our relationship with Christ is fairly, new. It is during those times that we have-to have a little talk with Jesus. We must to be able to discern His voice in order to follow His instruction. Not only had God shown me that He was the means by which my daughter would go to school. He let me know that I had nothing to do with where the funds would come from.

While I was praying for a listed scholarship, trying to get loans, even hoping to withdraw from my retirement to no avail. She was awarded a scholarship that had nothing to do with anything that I had ever applied for or even until this day, seen.

Be anxious for nothing,
But in everything by prayer and supplication,
With thanksgiving,
Let your requests be made known to God. *Philippians 4:6*

12

Passport

Now faith is the substance of things hoped for, the evidence of things not seen. For by it the elders obtained a good report. Hebrews 11

My oldest daughter got married on Saturday, September 26th, 2009. She and her high school sweetheart had one of the most exquisite weddings of the city. There were three hundred guests and a bridal party of twenty. People who were not invited were desperately trying to get invited. Everything from the wedding to the reception went extremely well as we all had prayed.

The honeymoon was to be spent in a luxury resort in Jamaica. Much time, effort and money had gone into the planning of this trip. The two were slated to fly out early that Monday morning around 7am.

My son in-law and daughter came to the house to pick

up something before they left for the airport. At some point we just happened to look at my son-in-law's passport and we discovered that the passport had expired. He thought that he had the most updated passport in his possession, but he was wrong. He had renewed his passport the year before, where he had proposed to my daughter on a family trip. They had only a couple of hours to get to the airport.

Neither of them had any idea where the passport could be. He went back to his parent's house to search the massive home for his passport. Meanwhile, my daughter was really letting him have it. She was panicking and rightfully so. He searched for about an hour and then came back to pick up my daughter. Someone had told him to drive to the airport and try to use the expired passport, if they could not use it, to reschedule the flight, drive to Chicago to get a passport in a day and then fly out the next day. Either way, major money was about to be lost not to mention that Chicago is four and a half hours away from Detroit.

I felt so sorry for my son-in-law because he could see the devastation in my daughter's face. He was hurt and I knew that he felt he had failed her terribly. They left to head for the airport, but deep in my heart I knew that it would be to no avail. My mother called with the bright idea that maybe, my son-in law had put his passport in daughter's luggage last year when we left Cancun. Her reasoning was that most of the time men give important items like that to their wives or girlfriends to put up for them.

I checked the luggage she used the previous year to no avail. As I walked pass the den, I noticed that it was 3:16am. I remembered thinking "Lord, we need a miracle." I said to the Lord, ok, you must want me to read John 3:16. But instead of reading John 3:16 at that time, I started looking through my daughter's wedding gifts and other stuff, for some hope of finding the passport. My hope was that maybe it had fallen into one of the gift bags or something. I knew deep down inside there would be no reason for it to be at my house. My daughter said that she had never handled his passport, so looking around that house was just a waste of time.

Eventually, I surrendered to the Lord's voice, located a bible and read *16For God so loved the world, that he gave his only begotten Son, that whosoever believeth in him should not perish, but have everlasting life (John 3:16).*

I read the scripture and proceeded to go upstairs to bed. Instead of making a right turn to my room I made a left to go to my newlywed daughter's bedroom just to sit on her bed. The room had years of college books, teacher books clothes, wedding magazines, boxes of shoes (hundreds) she is not a hoarder, but the room was in hoarder state because it had become a dumping ground over the last several years. There was literally nowhere to walk. I happened to find a corner of the bed amidst the junk in her room to just sit down and sigh. As I was sitting, I noticed a photo sticking out of the drawer of a plastic vanity most commonly used by college students for toiletries. Hair products from years gone by were piled on and in the vanity. As I was looking at one photo, I could see that there were more photos. I attempted to pull the drawer, but it was stuck.

As I yanked at the drawer, I saw that what was making the drawer stick was a passport. Chills ran up and down my spine as I opened the passport. There was no way possible that this could be his passport. It just was not possible. This vanity had not been used in at least two or three years and he had used the passport just a year ago. But it was there. I started screaming and running to find a phone to call them. They were on their way to the airport to cancel and reschedule the flight for their honeymoon.

When I got them on the phone they were screaming, my daughter said mom that is a miracle, his passport can't be there it is impossible for his passport to be there. My son in-law said in the background "your mom must have a pipeline to heaven." I told them to turn around and that we would meet midway. They had a very short time by which to make it to the airport to catch their original flight.

My screams startled my husband who had been in a deep sleep. He could not believe that I had found the passport. The other mother in-law was in disbelief. The grandmothers were in disbelief. I was repeating "I can't believe this; I can't believe this" and thanking God as I sped down the expressway in my robe.

As soon as I obeyed God's voice to read the scripture John 3:16, He led me to a needle in a haystack. If I had not stopped to sit on my daughter's bed, been intrigued by one picture in the midst of hundreds of pictures at 4 o'clock in the morning, a photo that was stuck in a drawer jammed by my son-in-law's passport!! Are you kidding? The voice of God is real! Because His voice is so loud and clear to me, my husband has often told me that I should start writing the experiences down. God has provided witnesses of these seemingly impossible events just as He did in biblical times. No matter how big, small or tumultuous the issue is, we can ask for

God's help and He will be there for us.

13

THE JOURNEY

A wise man will hear, and will increase learning; and a man of understanding shall attain unto wise counsels: Proverbs 1:5

I planned a road trip up north with my oldest daughter who at the time had an infant and a toddler. We were leaving our husband's home because I was determined that, yes I was fully capable of driving a long distance without the help of my "know it all" husband. I could do this, how dare he doubt my ability to make this happen. I was determined. A co-worker had offered up her cabin for any of us who wanted to make the trip that weekend. I told her that I would take her up on the offer.

My oldest daughter saw it as an opportunity to get "out of her four walls" and go, so she accepted the invitation to take the journey with me. Had I told her that I was going to Alaska, she would have been on board because she just loves to go, babies and all, leaving "the husband" as she calls him, at home. My coworker informed me that the cabin was in walking distance to the lake, that it was practically in her backyard. I love water, so the thought of being that close to a lake was more enticing than proving to my husband that I could indeed travel alone, that I would be fine without his presence.

We were supposed to get on the road by noon. By the time we packed, bought groceries changed the babies a couple of times, forgot stuff, ran errands and stopped for gas, it was early evening. We had a three- or four-hour drive ahead of us and I could not admit to my daughter, that I was nervous about driving at night to a place that I had never been, so I allowed pride to get the best of me.

About an hour and a half into the drive, we started to see lightening and hear thunder. Soon the rain was ferociously dancing on my windshield. I could not see very well at all but there was no way that I could tell my daughter that I was terrified. We drove for miles in the storm before we could find an exit that lead to a place of business. I decided that the best thing that I could do was to get a hotel room for the night. The first stop was an Inn of some sort. It did not appear to be inhabited by people at all, let alone completely booked. I did not believe a word that was coming out of the desk clerk's mouth. My daughter and I left in despair. Driving in the storm had turned dangerous for us because the rain was blinding. I was praying that the Lord would keep me from having an accident on this dark and dreary stretch of road. For as far as we could see there was nothing but trees and darkness. We were in Northern Michigan, a territory I had never travelled. The exits appeared to lead to nowhere and I did not want to end up in swampland, so I continued down the forbidden path hopefully to the intended destination.

I located the road and continued to drive. It took about two minutes for us to get so deep into the woods that we could barely see. The houses sat so far back, and the street signs were almost unintelligible. We found a driveway that was where the house was supposed to be. I slowly drove into the driveway to see if I could see an address, and yes this was the house. There was no front door evident. The lights from my car indicated that the door was probably around the back of the house, but it was surrounded by woods. There was no way possible that I was going to take the chance of getting my grandkids out of the car, safely up a staircase that appeared to lead to a dark and ominous hell. I just couldn't do it. Once we turned the car lights out, we would be at the mercy of the woods and all its carnivorous predators. Just thinking about this made my heart begin to fail. My daughter could sense my fear and she started to panic. The babies were crying by then. They were hungry and uncomfortable and startled by the uncertainty of it all. We had to leave. We had to find our way back to the main road, but I could not see behind us to back the Jaguar out of the driveway. There just was not enough light. After about fifteen minutes of inching backwards, I made it back onto the road, but I did not know which way to go. I did not know whether we came from the right or from the left or from north or the south. I was totally confused. We called the police. Someone answered the phone after several rings as if they were shut down for the night. When the dispatcher answered the phone, I asked her to please tell us how to get out of the maize that we were in. She could hear my daughter starting to scream at her from the back seat of the car, because the dispatcher was telling me to shut the babies up. I told her that they were babies, hungry, tired and wet and I could not shut them up.

My daughter started to scream at the person on the phone because she was totally annoyed, and she could not hold it in any longer. The lady dispatcher said that she would not help us because there was too much noise. I was literally in a twilight zone. In real life, police dispatcher's attempt to help people, at least that is what they do in the city.

We were in the country a world away from city life.

Even when I quieted my daughter, the lady could not help me determine which way to go. I began to pray. I had made this trip to prove a point to my husband and I had put my daughter and her children in danger when I decided to get on the road at night. I asked the Lord to please lead us out of this never ending, maize of woods back to the main road. I was petrified at the thought of running out of gas and eventually being surrounded by coyotes and bears or men who were up to no good. My daughter did not know that there was also the possibility that we could end up in the lake if we made the wrong turn.

I believe that this was the point at which my oldest daughter started to believe that I truly had a connection to God. Having no idea which way to turn, barely seeing what was before me because of the thickness of the woods, I made it back to the main road.

There were two hotels. The first one was a Holiday Inn. My daughter and I took the kids inside and tried to book a room. Again, no evidence of the hotel being booked to capacity and no other sign of life but the desk clerk. The clerk told us that the only room she had available was $499 per night. My daughter said to me "mom she is lying, she is lying!" I said to her, please calm down, we have the kids, you have to calm down. There is no way that I had $499 in my account. I just did not have it. So, even though I did not believe that the Holiday Inn could have a room worth $499 a night, I had to believe that it was going to work out for us. My God have never failed me yet. The clerk told us to go down the road, that there was another hotel that would probably have something available cheaper.

My daughter and I made the two-minute drive down the deserted road and there was an edifice that looked like something out of Night of the Living Dead. My daughter started crying. We knew that we could not get out of the car to go in. Not a single light was on, and the place wreaked of evil. I started praying to the Lord asking for His help and His guidance as I made my way back to the Holiday Inn, knowing that the most I had in my debit account was $150.00. The clerk did not even look up when I approached her. The Lord had spoken to her regarding us and she had to allow us to stay there. She just said to me, I have something for you, I can give it to you for $75. I thanked her. She gave us the key to the room. My daughter screamed when we opened the door to what she thought would be a substandard room. It was a huge suite with a chocolate oversized sectional, grand bluesy artwork, a stainless-steel kitchen, a king-sized bed and a jacuzzi. On the back of the door the rate $499 per night, was posted. I realized that I was trying to prove that I could do something that I had never done before to my husband, which would have been ok, but it was pride that motivated me to do it. I asked my daughter what lesson she learned that night. She replied, "I learned that I need to pray, have faith and trust in the Lord. He will make a way out of no way."

I did not want to go back home without having seen

the cabin my co-worker so graciously offered me. So, my daughter and I took a chance and drove the five miles into the woods to find the house. We realized just how impossible it would have been to make it up the back stairs which faced the woods, in the dead of night with two small children. But what was even more of a miracle, we happened upon the lake. If I had not been able to decipher the Lord's voice, leading me out of the conundrum, we would have driven to the lake and plunged to our death. There was no barrier, no warning signs, just an abyss a few yards from her home.

"5 Trust in the LORD with all thine heart; and lean not unto thine own understanding. 6 In all thy ways acknowledge him, and he shall direct thy paths." Proverbs 3:5-6

14
Laying on of Hands

[8] And the four beasts had each of them six wings about him; and they were full of eyes within: and they rest not day and night, saying, Holy, holy, holy, LORD God Almighty, which was, and is, and is to come. Revelation 4:8

We left our church of fourteen years as the Lord so lead my husband. We became members of a church which at the time had about four thousand members. It was pastored by a world-renowned anointed man of God.

On any given Sunday, the lower level of the sanctuary would be packed. You were not guaranteed a seat next to your family members if you did not arrive a little early. This Sunday in particular, our family was all over the church. The kids were either in the balcony with their cousins or sitting in the youth section. My husband and I had driven separate vehicles that day, which was not too uncommon because of our different engagements after church. At the onset of the service, I did not know whether he was there or not. I could not tell because of the massive amount of people.

Normally, I would sit as close to the front of the sanctuary as possible because I did not like sitting in the back under the balcony. I must have been a few minutes late because I found myself deep into the back portion of the sanctuary, but not quite under the balcony.

The praise was extremely high, and most people were bowing their head in prayer, while others were singing or speaking in tongues and the Pastor was speaking with great emotion and much profoundness.

As I kept my head bowed in prayer, a sudden feeling came over me that the Pastor was coming for me. God had placed in my spirit that the Pastor of this mega church was coming for me. There had to have been over a thousand people on the lower level that day. Pastor was moving about the congregation and his destination would be, me.

My head was bowed bracing myself for what was about to happen. Sure enough, the person next to me touched my arm and motioned for me to look up. I saw the Pastor standing in the aisle motioning for me to come out in the aisle. I excused myself past the people that were closest to the aisle and made my way.

The Pastor got on his knees bowing his head and began to pray loudly and fiercely over me. There was a minister and an alter worker in the aisle as well. I lifted my hands up towards the heavens and I did not say a word. I did not understand the concept of the laying on of hands at that time. But that was not my concern. I was just overwhelmed at the thought that I knew without the shadow of a doubt that the Pastor was coming for me. I was reverencing the Lord, crying and shaking my head in awe as once again, I had clearly heard the Lord say, that my Pastor was coming for me. As I drove over to my grandmother's house, I called my best friend out in Los Angeles to tell her what had happened.

Six or seven months passed, and I still did not know anything about the laying on of hands. I had not researched it, nor had I inquired about it from anyone in the last several months. One evening, I was in the kitchen making dinner. My husband was in his office preparing for his bible study class which was not associated with the ministry of the church we were attending at the time. Once again, God's still small voice told me to go talk to him about the laying on of hands. I was asking God to allow me to finish the dinner so that I could sit down, but his voice insisted that I stop what I was doing to go talk to my husband.

My husband and I had never discussed the events that took place that Sunday morning, so I did not even know for sure if he was there or not because of the size of the sanctuary. But I was obedient and heeded to God's voice. I went into my husband's office and asked him if he had seen what had happened to me that Sunday about six months earlier. He responded that he had indeed seen the Pastor lay hands on me. I proceeded to ask him what the laying on of hands meant. He clarified what the laying on of hands meant, but he also included that not all laying on of hands is of God. I did not quite know how to take that, but I responded by asking him when "was the last time someone had laid hands on you?" He said that it had been so long ago, that he could not remember.

The next day we both went our separate ways to work and after work activities. My husband would leave work on Tuesdays to attend bible study at our church, instead of going to lunch. He would return to work after bible study. That evening my husband came in the house saying, "you will never believe what happened to me today!" He said, "I opened the doors to the chapel, Pastor was already up teaching and as soon as I walked through the doors the Pastor motioned for me to come forward. I made my way to the front of the sanctuary, the Pastor laid hands on me and I fell out laying prostrate before God. I was shivering because of the conversation we had the night before, where you asked me the last time anyone had laid hands on me." Recalling what he had said to me the night before "all laying on of hands is not of God" I asked him, "was that laying on of hands, of God?" He was quiet.

God told me moments before the Pastor came to me, out of the couple thousand that were there that day, the Pastor was coming for me. It was an overwhelming sense of knowing without the shadow of a doubt, what was about to happen to me, that when it did, it just took my faith to another level. Six months later, after not having had any discussion about the incident whatsoever with my husband, God told me to talk to my husband about the laying on of hands. It was pressing that I interrupt making the sauce to my spaghetti to go talk to my husband, because I really did not want to stop what I was doing. But I had no choice. The very next day the Pastor did the same thing to my husband as he had done to me, six months earlier. My husband witnessed yet another time the unmistakable evidence of God's voice within my life. I am reminded of this scripture, *[14] Do not neglect the gift that is in you, which was given to you by prophecy with the laying on of the hands of the eldership (Timothy 4:14)*. Praise be to God.

Each of the incidents strengthened my faith and my desire for other people to listen for the sound of His voice. I never ask the question "why", because God is the answer to the "why" in all that I do and all that I am.

Faith is an attitude, a disposition of the nature of an individual who possesses it. I choose to believe God. I choose to believe that when I pay attention, I can hear His voice. I was at the table in my dining room when all of a sudden a youtube video came on with author and screen writer Shonda Rhymes. I was not looking her up nor was I looking up anything that had to do with her. The message of the video had to do with writing a book. She discussed how miserable she was after college, working a job that was not fulfilling to her and that she found solace in using her time at home to develop story lines and personalities for the books she saw

herself writing. Once again, the Lord stopped me dead in my

tracks to minister to me exactly what I was supposed to be

doing with my time. I have spent so much of my life hating

that I did not know how to get to working on my book

because of the ever present clutter of everything else in my

life, that the thought of never being able to get to it, consumed

me.

My son Sidney, made me promise in December of 2017

to finish the book by the end of the month. I remember

thinking, Lord, I just need to add one more miracle to the

book before calling it complete. What was about to transpire

in my life could not have been predicted. Again, there would

be hundreds of witnesses to this miracle which would directly

affect the climate of my workplace as well as the direction of

the district.

15

The Bait

The Son of man shall send forth his angels, and they shall gather out of his kingdom all things that offend, and them which do iniquity;
Matthew 13:41

One of my very best friends and spiritual confidant's is a teacher and co-worker of mine. We both needed to have foot surgery and since it was the end of the year, she suggested that I go to her doctor to get the surgery done before the deductible started over. I figured I could take the time off work following a two week off vacation from school during the Christmas Holidays. I would return by the end of January, missing only a couple of weeks of school and I would be back at the change of the semester, which in High School is important.

A couple of Sunday's before the surgery, a lady at my church mentioned the book "Bait of Satan" by John Bevere, to me. It caught me off guard because it was one of the first books my women's department read. This lady was not a member of my church at that time, so there was no way for her to know that the book was of special interest to me. I asked her what made her say that to me, and she just responded that she was reading the book with a group. I made it up in my mind that I would go to the bible bookstore and get the book again to revisit it with my lady membership. I wrote the date February 10, 2018 in the book with a message that I am just seeing today, January 3, 2019 that states, "2nd time reading." The Lord knew that I needed this date back then, but I did not know that I would ever need it. I simply followed the guidance of the holy spirit and wrote the date down.

Prior to the discussion about having foot surgery with my friend and coworker, the principal had been trying to intimidate me with her words and suggestive comments. I did not understand why, could not fathom in my head any kind of purpose whatsoever for her to treat me that way. I had met her briefly some sixteen years prior when she was assistant principal at the school where three of my children attended. Her daughter attended the school at the same time. I don't ever recall meeting her daughter, but she played sports.

Whenever the principal would speak to me it was regarding a student who was not doing well in my AP literature class. The student was absent a lot and when she was present her work was substandard. The principal would say to me "we have to meet about that young lady in your class who wants her grade changed, you know that our babies can't do this work, your kids went to "ABC" School. The comment about our students not being capable of doing what other teens are expected to do rubbed me the wrong way first of all because, I figured that if it has already been decided that my students can't do the work, why I am bothering trying to teach them. The statement about my kids attending a different school was meant to say that they were in a different environment and that the expectations were higher; suggesting that our students lacked the capacity to do the work. The principal would make that same statement three different times to me before the Christmas break. The last statement she made to me was over the phone from her office. She spoke very loudly so that anyone else in the office could hear her. She was trying to intimidate me once again in front of an audience. I left my classroom and went to the union rep whose classroom I had never been to before to tell him that I was tired of the principal harrassing me and I did not want to have further contact with her without union representation present.

The school would be out for two weeks and my surgery was scheduled for two days after Christmas. I made sure that I supplied sub work for at least six weeks. I had taken work home to grade and I continued to grade the work from the sub to make sure that my students got the grade they deserved come the middle of January which marked the end of the 1st semester. When my grades were complete, I submitted the 1st semester grades as I had always done.

I was online one day while trying to recooperate from surgery and I saw that my principal was reaching out to me to change a student's grades who had been skipping my class and had not done the work. I knew that this young lady was skipping my class but there was nothing that I could do about it. I messaged the principal that the young lady earned the grade she received and that there was no reason for me to change the grade at that point. The student had simply failed to do the work.

The following Monday, I received a call from one of my students. She said that there was some lady in my room packing my belongings saying that I was not going to return and if I did, I would be teaching the 9th grade. I had been teaching juniors and senior AP literature for some time. I could not believe what I was hearing. Other students started calling me and eventually the teachers started calling me asking if I had quit. I went online to check the student's grades and sure enough the principal had changed all the grades in my AP Lit class to reflect something that was not true. She thought that she could get away with it by switching me to ninth grade moving me to another part of the building where my former students would have little to no access to me.

Meanwhile my husband and I had made it to the bible bookstore to get the book "Bait of Satan." I looked around the store to the area where the book should have been. to no avail. When I got to the counter, I asked the cashier if they still carried the book. He said to me, it is right here. He handed the book to me from the counter as if it was sitting there for me. My husband went to pull the car to the front of the store to pick me up because I was still on crutches. When I got into the car, I opened the book randomly to page 43. The subtitle was "Is God Using Me to Expose My Leader's Sins" I was in such shock that I showed my husband. All week I had been talking about exposing my principal for what she had done. This subtitle appeared to give me the go ahead to do just that. However, once I read the chapter, I realized that it was just the opposite. The question that ended the chapter was "Will you be a man or woman after the heart of God, or will you seek to avenge yourself (Bevere, 47)?" At that point, I knew that seeking to destroy her to avenge myself was not going to be the answer.

Once I returned to work, the principal told me that I could not have one of the empty rooms in the wing that I was transferred from even though the rooms were nice, clean and updated. Instead she had my boxes transferred to a room that had a brick wall blocking the board from the students. In the back area of the room was a dank smell coming from molded carpet. I was to share this room with the acting teacher. She told the acting teacher I was there temporarly and she told me that I would be there permanently. I am an English teacher, so to teach in a room designed to teach acting did not make sense even to the students. There was a wall blocking the view of the board, from the students. I could not unpack my twenty-three boxes of papers and notes and books and records and settle in to teach my one hundred and fifty students. The drama teacher would not pack her items to leave because she was told that I was there on a temporary basis. Both of us were uncomfortable and it made for an unhealthy work enviroment.

I ended up having six asthma attacks the first week of my return alone because of the mold. I had not had an asthma attack in two years, so I did not even have an inhaler on me. One attack was so bad that a teacher started to pray for me while I was having the attack. I refused to continue teaching the students in a room where I would not teach my own children. I would teach them in the cafeteria or any clean area I could find, but not that room.

Eventually, an administrator allowed me to teach my students in her room because she only needed it for professional development meetings. The principal had a problem with that because the room was too nice. Because I would have no conversation with the principal, another administrator found a room for me. The harrassment against me was having an affect on the girls' mentoring program that I sponsored and had sponsored for many years. It was and still is known as an upstanding program where the young ladies learn how to give back to the community, become great leaders and positive role models.

The last straw for me was that the principal would not release funds to the girls that they had earned. She had denied them field trips, fundraisers and practically everything that they wanted to do but would lie to them and tell them that she was working on it. I finally had to tell them that she was doing this to hurt me, and that I was so sorry because it was really hurting them.

My oldest son who lives out of state was not aware of what had been happening to me with his former assistant principal. He happened to ask me how I was doing, this must have been early May. I told him I wasn't having chest pain anymore because of Ms. Principal. He said "Mom, wait. Before you tell me anything else…it is my fault." I asked him what he was talking about. He revealed to me that when he was in high school, Miss Principal called him to her office and badgered him to date her daughter. I was livid. I could not believe what I was hearing. My son was now 32 years old and I was not aware that she had tried to intimidate him, all those years ago. For me to find out that this lady had used her authority over my son to try to make him date her daughter was just appalling to me.

But it all started to make sense. She had a vendetta against me because my son did not like her daughter over sixteen years ago. At that point, it took everything in me not to expose her, but because of what I had read in Bait of Satan, I was not sure of what to do.

I prayed that the Lord would allow me to finish the school year without doing something that I would regret. I knew that this lady tried to publicly humiliate me, and all of my co-workers knew it. What I did not know was that there were other teachers being harassed, but they were afraid to speak up.

I would later find out how many teachers were privately suffering but were too afraid of losing their jobs to say anything. The last go around would be Ms. Principal denying my mentoring program the use of money for a field trip, that they had earned during a school event. We had been promised that the girls would have access to the money prior to the end of the school year because most of them were graduating. They had assisted another organization in raising money, and they were promised that they would be able to reap the rewards of their labor. I could no longer take it. Before I pressed the send button, I made sure that I had no regrets and I felt in my heart that the Lord had my back. I was prepared to be fired or to go to jail to stand up for what rightfully belonged to my students. My email response to her denial of my request to use the funds that the girls rightfully

earned was:

Your question "what is the instructional value for the activity"

I. The instructional value for the activity is that when you invest your time and money into something, there will often be payoffs

2. The instructional value for the activity is that student organizations will be treated fairly and not discriminated against just because the administrator has a problem with the sponsor.

3. The instructional value for the activity is that students won't be cheated out of their rewards by administrators who don't care to understand what the organization is all about in the first place

4. The instructional value is that this is an after-school program not an academic class!

5. The instructional value is that honesty has always been the best policy. Say what you mean and mean what you say.

6. The instructional value is that you don't use the hard work and efforts of students to bully another person because their son would not date your daughter 16 years ago. You called him in the office to intimidate him when he was only a teenager and you were his administrator. I just found out.

7. The instructional value is that what is done in the dark will come to the light.

8. The instructional value is that my heavenly Father orders my steps!

I sent this email out to the entire staff. I told my close friend and coworker to read her email. I told her that I was in my class waiting for the police to come to my room and handcuff me. Teachers started knocking on my door asking me if I meant to send the email to the entire staff. I told them that it was done intentionally. The visits by teachers continued. Each teacher told me that they had my back and several of them shared their stories of how this lady had made their lives a living hell. I could not believe what I was hearing. Teachers shared that she had made them cry, had made them feel less than worthy of being a teacher, that she had made intimidating statements to them. I was even told that other administrators were filing grievances against her. There are over a hundred teachers at the highschool and a third of them had filed or were looking to file grievances against this lady. While the dirt done to them was private, what was done to me was very public. I did not end up getting arrested for sending the email but I had to meet with the district lawyer, the superintendent of instruction and several union reps the day before the last day of school.

The district lawyer was shocked that the principal had changed a whole class's grades to all A's even though they had not earned it. The principal had plagiarized report cards under the notion that I would not find out. The union representatives, the attorney and the administrator left the room. Only one person returned. The next day which was the last day of school, someone said to me as I was about to leave the buidling, "did you hear, she quit." I asked who, they replied, "Ms.Principal, she quit." At the time of writing this miracle, the first year without Ms. Principal is coming to a close. The bondage and the chains have been lifted from the people. Last year, the students from the ninth grade to the twelfth grade hated school. It was evident in the constant local news reports of fighting and the lack of transparency on the administration. Teachers who were never absent were missing work every other Friday. There would be so many teachers absent that there were never enough substitutes. Teachers were just quitting or transferring in the middle of the terms which was unheard of in this district. The current principal has changed the climate to one of respect, nurturing and concern for the well being of the students, teachers and the staff. The hallways have an air of peace about them. I am reminded,

"For we wrestle not against flesh and blood, but against principalities, against powers, against the rulers of the darkness of this world, against spiritual wickedness in high places." Ephesians 6:12

16

Wisdom Words

Be true to who you are. If you find yourself approaching enviousness towards someone, ask for the Lord to rid you of that feeling. Instead recognize the beauty or the gift as something that the Lord gave them. The thought will keep you from disregarding the fact that God blesses who He pleases. There is no room for envy in the mind of someone who loves the Lord and wants to please Him. Stop complaining. Complaining is finding fault. Our Lord and Savior was too busy about His Father's business to concentrate on the mumbling and complaining. He did not have time to sew discord. He knew that his walk on this earth was limited.

Knowing that our days are numbered without knowing

the end date is what gets people in trouble. We always feel as if we will have one more day to get it right. But one day we will be wrong. Most of us will not have a warning that this is our last day or hour.

How many chances will we have been given before the blinds are shut the draperies drawn?

You survived that abusive relationship because God has plans for you. The death of your child took your desire to live, but there is something that the Lord still wants you

to do. You don't know how you will make ends meet, but somehow you still exist, He is waiting on you. Your dreams seem to fail, over and over again, but God is trying to tell

you something. Listen. You are depressed when you should feel blessed and you don't know why. He is trying to hold your hand. The sins of your biological father have cursed you, but your deliverance is a prayer away. You want a relationship with Him, but you deny Him access to you, because you remain in sin. Choose ye this day whom you will serve.

17

✔ Your Spirit

- Start the meeting with prayer end the meeting with prayer. Prayer holds all involved accountable.

- If someone can't look you in the eyes when talking to you about things that matter, your light is too bright, and it is imposing on a dark place within them.

- I did not pray about the millions that they stood to earn, I prayed about the miracles by which they would learn... about God's grace. (40YOG)

- Integrity is priceless, the lack of it is expensive.

- A clean heart welcomes the guidance of the Holy Spirit.

- Jealousy and envy are evil products, return them quickly.

- A prideful spirit disrespects God and dishonors truth. It is the great pretender.

- Examine your motives. Is God pleased?

- When the Lord gives you direction, don't take another route.

- Speak life.

- Recognize the goodness in people, the favor will be returned.

- Bless those who curse you.

- Praise God for the rain.

- Read your bible,

- Pray, then trust God.

- Find a quiet place, listen.

- Breathing is a reason to celebrate!

18

Level Up

Level Up: 17 Steps to Clear the Clutter

1. Find a place preferably within your home with minimal distractions.

2. Look out of the window in the evening and focus on the sky, the stars or even the rain.

3. During the day, witness the branches of trees dancing in the breeze.

4. Drive to a nearby pond and focus on the subtle motion of the water.

5. Listen to the sound of a running waterfall online.

6. If you are near a river or lake, fix your eyes on the rhythm of the waves.

7. Sit on the porch for a few minutes, be still and inhale.

8. Contemplate that you are here for God's purpose. Relax.

9. Walk and pray, Your will Lord, Your will Lord.

10. Marvel at your blessings.

11. Expect a Word from the Lord.

12. Celebrate a miracle.

13. Listen.

14. Thank God for who He is.

15. Prepare your heart to bless someone today.

16. Rebuke negative thoughts.

17. Pay attention to the "coincidences." God is trying to tell you something.

19
Angel of CHANGE

Now that you have the steps for clearing the clutter, take action to make a difference in the lives of others. A change angel deliberately seeks to honor the Lord, serve the Lord and bless the Lord with his whole heart daily.

- Ask the Lord in prayer, to lead you to the right church to join.

- Give the Lord your all as you serve on an auxiliary. Pay Tithes.

- Respect the spiritual leaders that you chose to assist you in your spiritual walk. If you don't' respect them, leave, examine yourself and pray for them.

- Prepare to be a blessing and not a curse, every day of your life.

- Use your spiritual or natural gifts to bless people in some way.

- Take the focus off what is wrong in your life to make something right in someone else's, you will reap rewards. Become an angel of change.

- Raise awareness about an issue or illness. (hunger, abuse, adoption)

- Volunteer to read to children, sit with the elderly or clean a play area or neighborhood.

- Check on a neighbor who is aging or ill or just alone, pray with them.

- Start a mentoring program, for kids, women or men.

- Fundraise for challenged groups.

- Teach computer skills to a senior citizen while witnessing to them.

- Join the PTA where your child attends school.

- Start a prayer group in your neighborhood or at your place of employment.

- Go on a spiritual retreat at least once a year.

- Babysit for a mother or father who needs a break.

- Say the words "Have a blessed day" to everyone, as you depart.

I will bless the LORD at all times: his
praise shall continually be in my mouth.
Psalm 34:1

For Angel Retreats or Waterfall Workshops
Go to:
AngelsandWaterfalls.com

Contact:
Darcel Stewart
AngelsandWaterfalls@gmail.com

Made in the
USA
Monee, IL

14055161R00083